FUN with the VIOLIN

CONTENTS

This is a collection of level 1, E-Z violin solos. All of the solos in this text may be played *together* in *ensemble* with the Fun With Viola, Fun With Cello, and Fun With Bass books. These texts were written as an ideal supplement to any string method.

1 2 3 4 5 6 7 8 9 0

© Copyright 1971   Mel Bay Publications, Inc., Pacific, Mo.
International Copyright Secured
All rights reserved   Printed in U.S.A.

THE VIOLIN

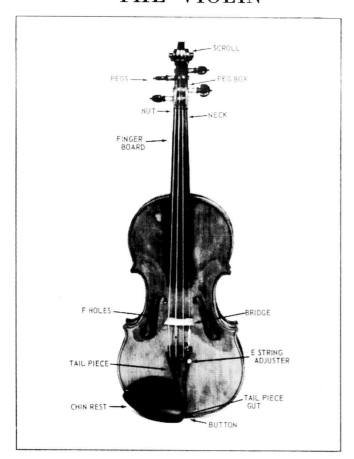

THE BOW

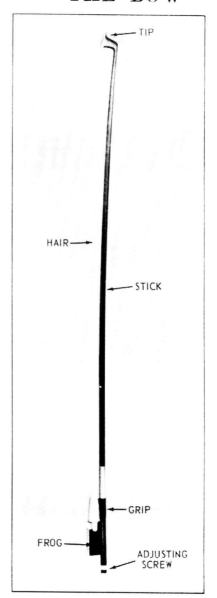

TUNING THE VIOLIN

First String . . . . E
Second String . . . . A
Third String . . . . D
Fourth String . . . . G

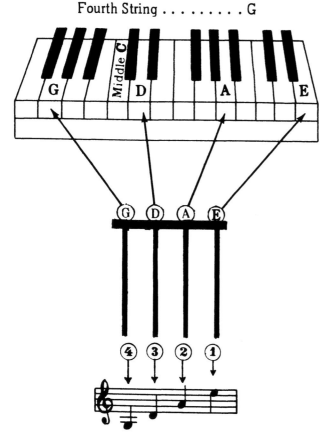

PITCH PIPES

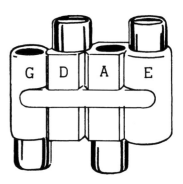

A Pitch Pipe for the Violin may be purchased from any music store. Each pipe will have the correct pitch for each Violin string. A Pitch Pipe is a valuable aid.

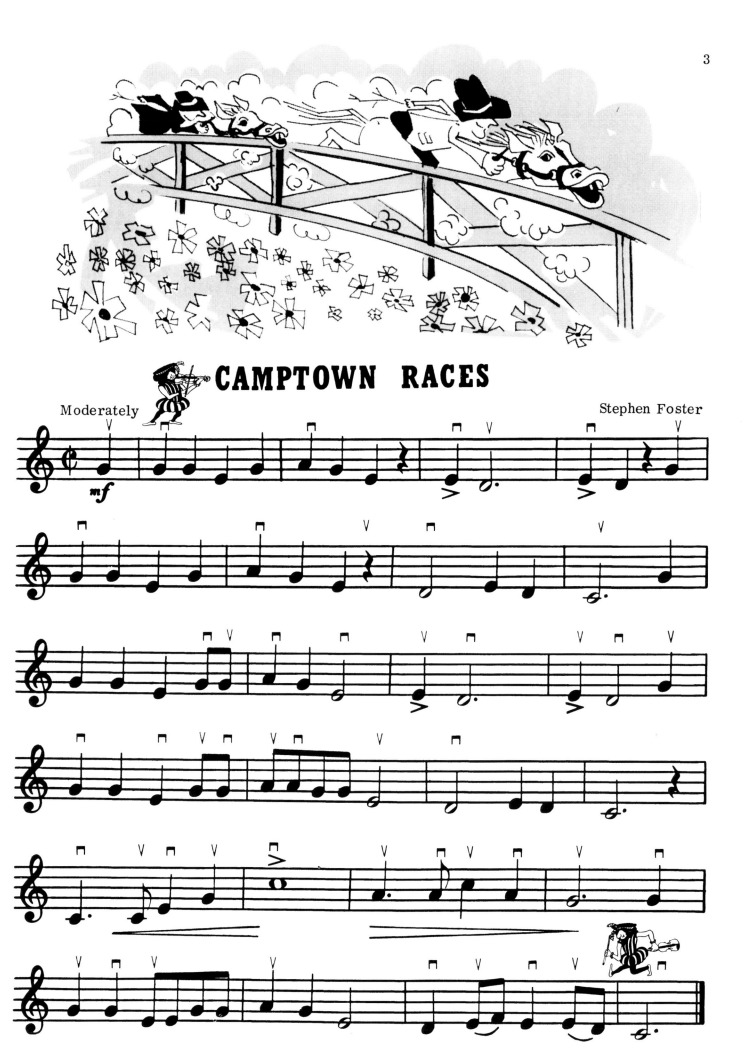

CAMPTOWN RACES

Stephen Foster

Moderately

Copyright 1971 Mel Bay Publications, Inc.
International Copyright Secured Printed in USA

When The Saints Go Marching In

Traditional

Black Is The Color Of My True Love's Hair

Folk Song

BLOW THE MAN DOWN

Sea Chanty

Michael Row The Boat Ashore

Moderately

Spiritual

RED RIVER VALLEY

Slowly

Cowboy Song

Drink To Me Only With Thine Eyes

Traditional

8

TOM DOOLEY

Moderately

mf

Folk Song

ALOUETTE

Brightly

mf

French Song

AURA LEE

Traditional

STREETS OF LAREDO

Cowboy Song

OH! SUSANNA

American Folk Song

Blue Bells Of Scotland

Scotch Folk Song

Look Down That Lonely Road

Spiritual

MY BONNIE

Moderately

Traditional

mf

Chorus

The Eyes Of Texas

Brightly

Traditional

THE ERIE CANAL

Brightly

Traditional

I've Been Working On The Railroad

Traditional

COCKLES AND MUSSELS

LOCH LOMOND

HOME ON THE RANGE

Cowboy Song

WAYFARIN' STRANGER

Folk Song

She'll Be Comin' 'Round The Mountain

Traditional

GREENSLEEVES

Slowly

Old English Song

HATIKVOH

Hebrew National Anthem

GYPSY LAMENT

Gypsy Folk Song

Bill Bailey Won't You Please Come Home

Bright, With A Beat

Dixieland

Battle Hymn Of The Republic

Julia Ward Howe

SHORTNIN' BREAD

Traditional

COME BACK TO TORINO

Francesco Carlo Zucco

Swing Low, Sweet Chariot

SANTA LUCIA

Neapolitan Song

LONDONDERRY AIR

Slowly

Traditional

rit.

Down By The Riverside

With a strong beat

Traditional

Fine

Chorus

D.C. 𝄋 al Fine

Hail Hail The Gang's All Here

Moderately

Traditional

26

DIXIE

When Johnny Comes Marching Home

Traditional

THIS TRAIN

Brightly

Spiritual

THE DRUNKEN SAILOR

Brightly   Sea Chanty

I GAVE MY LOVE A CHERRY

Slowly   Folk Song

SHENANDOAH

Folk Song

CAPE COD CHANTY

Sea Chanty

JOHN HENRY

Brightly

Folk Song

Old Shoe Boots And Leggins

Brightly

Traditional

It Takes A Worried Man

Brightly

Folk Song

Chorus

FINE

D.S. 𝄋 al Fine

THE ENTERTAINER THEME

Scott Joplin